Life, Love and Beyond

Heidemarie Wawrzyn

Life, Love and Beyond

Bibliografische Information der Deutschen Nationalbibliothek:
Die Deutsche Nationalbibliothek verzeichnet diese Publikation in der
Deutschen Nationalbibliografie; detaillierte bibliografische Daten
sind im Internet über http://dnb.dnb.de abrufbar.

© 2019 Wawrzyn, Heidemarie

Herstellung und Verlag:
BoD - Books on Demand, Norderstedt, Germany

ISBN: 9783750400986

Table of Contents

This little book is dedicated
to anyone who reads it.

Author, Jerusalem, June 2018

A Gift from Heaven

A gift from heaven opened up like a fountain.

It guided me to an inner field of creativity

To a spring of sparkling thoughts and ideas

And hidden feelings of beauty, light and quiet

To express my moods, needs and views,

To heal my inner void, to make me feel whole.

Picture Gallery

Silence – beauty - and impressive artwork,
An almost holy atmosphere.

Paintings of former centuries,
Picasso, Renoir, Brueghel, Caspar D. Friedrich.

I am walking through the halls of a gallery
Surrounded by painted memories and emotions.

(Written after a visit to the picture gallery at the Israel Museum in
Jerusalem)

They touch my skin; they enter my heart.

Each painting seems to be alive, full of energy.

What a difference to a modern flat screen!

Its pictures sharp and bright, but cold.

The gallery's paintings are alive.

They speak to me and make me feel.

They provide a glimpse into bygone moments.

The Quiet of the Desert

No cars, no radio, no iPhones,
No music, no noise, no chats,
Only wind, sand, and mountains
And the quiet of the desert.

Sitting on a solid rock,
I set my mind to rest.
I listen to the cosmic music:
The quiet of the desert.

I can hear it all around me.
I can touch it like a breeze.
I can feel it deep inside me:
The quiet of the desert.

It makes me hear my secret thoughts,
It helps me touch my hopes and dreams,
It makes me enter my inner source of creativity,
The quiet of the desert.

On the Road:
From Eilat to Jerusalem, April 2019

I am Happy

I am not rich or well known.

I don't have any real estate or a promising career.

I don't have a huge family with siblings and nieces.

Nonetheless, I feel happy.

I feel happy because I live in a country I love.

I feel happy because I have a job I like.

I feel happy because I have friends

Who opened up an entirely new world to me.

A Moment of Happiness

Sometimes –

All of a sudden,

A stream of positive energy enters my body.

It flows through my brain, my heart, my emotions.

Sometimes –

All of a sudden,

That stream fills me with a vibrant sense of being

Alive with new ideas, thoughts and love.

At such a moment,

I feel close to everybody and everything,

To life, to death and to the entire universe.

The entire world inside me.

An Ocean of Tears

An ocean of tears
Overflows my emotions.
An ocean of tears
Begins to flood my soul.

A picture appears before my inner eye:
A forest in winter,
Trees without leaves,
Grass without color.

From afar, I hear rolling trucks,
The weeping of children,
The wailing of women,
The silent protest of fathers.

Soon the army trucks will arrive,
Spit out their load without mercy,
Turn the forest into a field of death.
And leaving an ocean of tears inside me.

S O M E ....

Sometimes

I love life.

I hate life.

Sometimes

It tastes bitter.

It tastes sweet.

Sometimes

Life seems endless.

Life seems fleeting.

.... **T I M E S**

Life is everything.

Ein Gedi, Kibbutz Hotel

The Purpose of Life

What is the purpose of life?

       A great career?

       Founding a family?

       Building a house?

       Making lots of money?

Or just being a being?

       - A part of nature

       - A petal in a field of flowers

       - A wave in an endless ocean

       - A dot in the Circle of Eternity

Mesila Train Track Park, Jerusalem

Different Ways of Life

Growing up in a Pietistic Christian home,
Educated in the spirit of the Ten Commandments,
I definitely learned honesty and discipline:
"Pray and labor!"

Getting in touch with Judaism in Germany
And later on, with Reform Judaism in Israel,
I joyfully embraced the variety of opinions:
Deed over Creed.

Encountering the beauty of Islamic artwork
And feeling touched by the music of the Sufis,
I deeply inhaled what Islamic art embodies:
Beauty and Harmony.

Falling in Love with You

I look into your eyes and see thousands of little sparks

Like shooting stars falling from heaven into my heart.

I look into your eyes and see a crystal-clear mountain lake

Harboring clandestine treasures and magic thoughts.

I look into your eyes and see a secret golden mirror,

Reflecting your inner picture of me.

I look into your eyes and see beautiful, warm lights.

I feel the strong desire to lose myself in your eyes.

(Inspired by Sufi poetry: Hafiz and Rumi).

Dance, Dance, Dance, a Dream

Our souls,

Two little bright lights,

Met last night.

We danced and danced

Until the end of the night.

Our souls,

Two little bright lights,

Said goodbye at dawn.

We returned to our daily life

With the rising of the sun.

Broken Loves

How many broken loves
Can a human being bear?

One strong love died through betrayal.
Another by selfish grasping.
A beautiful fine love fell slowly asleep.

How can I fill the void?
How can I replenish the emptied space?
How can I return from desert to life?

Will I be able to forget the pain?
Overcome the fear of getting hurt?
Get the strength to risk again?

Eilat, Red Sea, Broken Mermaid

Unemployed

Unemployed through the night

Until a new idea arises,

Clear and bright.

Job – part-time, full-time – or just a sabbatical?

Research, write, or create a book,

Life is like a musical.

Unemployed through the night

Until a new idea arises,

Clear and bright.

Separation

Separation supports growth.

Separation leads to freedom.

Separation creates more space.

Separation opens new doors.

Separation is life.

Inspired by Maryam Mafi: "A Little Book of Mystical Secrets. Rumi, Shams of Tabriz, and the Path of Ecstasy" (Charlottesville: Hampton Roads Publishing, 2017, pp. 13f).

Jerusalem-Baka, March 2018

Mother Nature

Mother Nature is both in one:

Gentle and harsh,

Taking and giving,

Challenging and comforting.

Dreaming of Paradise

Up in the mountains,

Just Mother Nature and me.

A beautiful hilly landscape in front of me,

A comforting silence all around.

        Up in the mountains,

        Just God's world and me.

A simple hut my cozy home,
Birds and cats my companions.

Up in the mountains,
Just the life I long for:
Quiet, peace, and serenity,
United with the universe.

China, Sichuan, 2014
(Courtesy of Anonymous)

Inspirations of a Landscape

It is nature

That made me feel what it is to be human

And part of the landscape at the same time.

It is nature

That made me see and understand,

That we were once part of it,

Beautiful, like the grass, the flowers, the clouds.

It is nature

That took me back to that point in my soul,

Beautiful, deep, mortal and immortal

At the same time.

Idea by Anonymous, edited by Heidemarie Wawrzyn

Nature Comes and Goes

Nature is older than any culture and religion.

It is closer to the first day of creation.

Nature follows the mysterious cycle of life,

Comes and goes, mends and never ends.

We are not more and not less than a bird in the sky,

A leaf in the wind and a drop in the ocean.

We are part of the beautiful, eternal cycle of life.

We come and go, mend and never end.

What Makes me Happy?

When I sit in a beautiful place
Surrounded by a breathtaking landscape,
I sense the quiet of the moment,
The peacefulness around me.
I feel like a part of nature,
Like an element within the universe.

When I sit in a beautiful place
Surrounded by a breathtaking landscape,
I feel like a witness to something divine,
Something mysterious and timeless,
Something for now and forever.
I wish this moment of happiness would never end.

About the Author

Heidemarie Wawrzyn grew up in Berlin, Germany and studied History of Religions at the University of Bremen. In 1998, she received a doctorate degree for her research on antisemitism in the early German women's movement.

A few months later, in 1999, she moved to Jerusalem, where she worked at different German and Jewish institutes. She became a postdoctoral researcher at the Hebrew University of Jerusalem in 2001 and a freelance transcriber of old German handwritten documents. Until her retirement in 2016, she was employed by the L. A. Mayer Museum for Islamic Art in Jerusalem.

It was not until 2014 that she started writing poetry. "Life, Love and Beyond" is the author's third collection of poems. .

List of Pictures:

Page 8:   Photo of author, Jerusalem, 2018.
             Courtesy of Donna Schatz,
             photographer and filmmaker,
             Richmond, Virginia, USA.

Page 34   China, Sichuan, 2014.
             Courtesy of Anonymous.

All other images were taken from the author's private photo collection.